DAY AND SWING TRADING

Guide for beginners.
Investment strategies in stock, options, and forex. Add up extra income and get your financial freedom

MARK BROKER

© **Copyright 2020 - All rights reserved.**

The content contained within this book may not be reproduced, duplicated or transmitted without direct written permission from the author or the publisher.

Under no circumstances will any blame or legal responsibility be held against the publisher, or author, for any damages, reparation, or monetary loss due to the information contained within this book. Either directly or indirectly.

Legal Notice:

This book is copyright protected. This book is only for personal use. You cannot amend, distribute, sell, use, quote or paraphrase any part, or the content within this book, without the consent of the author or publisher.

Disclaimer Notice:

Please note the information contained within this document is for educational and entertainment purposes only. All effort has been executed to present accurate, up to date, and reliable, complete information. No warranties of any kind are declared or implied. Readers acknowledge that the author is not engaging in the rendering of legal, financial, medical or professional advice. The content within this book has been derived from various sources. Please consult a licensed professional before attempting any techniques outlined in this book.

By reading this document, the reader agrees that under no circumstances is the author responsible for any losses, direct or indirect, which are incurred as a result of the use of information contained within this document, including, but not limited to, — errors, omissions, or inaccuracies.

TABLE OF CONTENT

INTRODUCTION 1
1. DIFFERENCE BETWEEN SWING TRADING AND DAY TRADING 4
2. HOW DOES IT WORK? 13
What is swing trading? 13

How does it work? 13
How to make swing trade with trends? 14
Tips for Beginners 15
Trading Platforms 17
What is day trading? 18

How does day trading work? 18
How to make day trade with trends? 20
Tips for Beginners 21
Trading Platforms 23
3. SWING TRADING AND DAY TRADING: TACTICS AND STRATEGIES. 26
What is strategy? 26

How many strategies does a trader need? 27
Types of strategies: 27
Day trading strategy 28

Important Components for day trading: 30
How much risk is involved in day trading? 31
Day Trading Strategies 34

Strategies 34
Application 40
Limit Your Losses 41
Forex Trading Strategies 41
Swing trading strategy 42

What is a swing trader? 42

Popular Swing Trading Strategies: 45
Forex Swing Trading Strategies: 45
Improving swing trading strategies for beginners: 47
Managing risk in Forex swing trading: 48
Swing trading money management: 50
The best tools for swing trading: 51
Top tips for Forex swing trading for beginners: 53
Choose a Broker for Forex Swing: 55

Forex Swing Trading Strategies 56

A Summary 56
Admiral Markets: 57

4. SWING AND DAY TRADING INDICATORS 58

What are the indicators of trading? 58

Why Are Technical Indicators Important? 58

Types of Technical Indicators 59

Swing Trading Indicators: 62
Day Trading Indicators: 68
Should You Trade on Technical Indicators? 71

5. PROS AND CONS OF SWING AND DAY TRADING 73

Advantages of Swing Trading 73

Disadvantages of Swing Trading 74

Advantages of Day Trading: 76

CONCLUSION 81

INTRODUCTION

In this book, we will talk about two types of trading: day trading and swing trading. It is necessary for every beginner to understand both sections. In order to start your career as a successful trader, you should have some basic knowledge about trading. This book will help you to clarify your doubts regarding day trading and swing trading. This guide will show to the beginners how they should invest their money and which trade will give them more profit.

Day trading is defined as the activity of capturing profit from the variation of stock prices during the day. In other words, day trading is about selling and buying stocks in a short time.

On the other side, swing trading is defined as the activity of buying and selling stocks during a time span of more than one day.

"Trading" is intended as the set of actions aimed to making extra-income money through investment strategies. Those who apply trading strategy in the financial market for gaining profit and helding a position in the market are known as "Swing Traders." Swing traders typically focus on getting profit by small gains in a very short time span. Their position in the market may be held for several days or for a week. They buy some stocks on the market and then sell them when they believe they can get a good profit on it. It is a process going on between a buyer and a seller. Swing traders keep their check and balance in the market; then, with the help of technical analysis, they identify the price swings and determine whether buy a stock or not, whether prices are rising, or they can come out with a loss. Swing traders risk 0.5% on each trade; nevertheless they pursue much higher goals in terms of profit by each trade. Most of the traders buy the stock when they prices are low and sell them when the prices are higher in the market. In some cases, this strategy causes losses, because the stock values decrease (this happens in very rare cases, though).

Most people make confusion between swing trading with day trading. In reality, swing trading is far different from day trading because day trading has lower chances of getting losses than swing trading. Also, in day trading, the time of trading is limited (one day), whereas in swing trading there is no time limit: it is indeed an overnight process. The market of swing traders works for 24hours; therefore, the profit/loss chances are higher because the seller can face the downfall anytime. Swing traders are also rewarded by a leverage of 50%. For example, if a trader is allowed to have a margin in his trading, then he only needs to invest $20,000 for a trade rather than investing $40,000. It is a process through which it is possible to helding profit for a long time. This process is not about getting profit in a day, but it could go from a day to many days. There will be more chances of getting profit than loss. For beginners, swing trading is the best option to choose because swing trading is easy and there are more chances of succeed with it. It is, in fact, less stressful for a seller and it is associated to higher success probability with respect to day trading, since time allows to improve accuracy in investment decision. It is well known that swing traders have several opportunities and options to trade. They may get more opportunities to invest their money during the longer investment time-span. It is very important for a trader be concerned in the price variation of their stock and be patient. After all, everything is all about profit and loss.

The main objective of this book is to help the beginners in trading and to teaching about the day and swing trading. So far, all the websites or books about day and swing trading that I have been reading were unfit to a clear understanding of how to enter or exit in any trading system. I wrote this book so that it will help the coming generations to understand what day and swing trading are about, and investing their money on the type of trading that suits better to them.

1. DIFFERENCE BETWEEN SWING TRADING AND DAY TRADING

If you are a beginner, then keep your mind open for both types of trading, do not waste your money or time in investing until you do not have enough knowledge about the trading systems. For a beginner, there is always a lot of things to learn about, whatever the field is learning about your interest is very important. Before starting any trading pattern, it is necessary to understand your needs and expectations that you have related to the trading system. First of all, the trader who wants to trade should know how much active trading he wants. Whether he wants a trading system that survives in the market for a longer time, or not. What are his current requirements and expectations related to trading whether he can handle his trading system for a long time, or did he have enough stamina to bear the loss? Once you decide the right path that suits you and that you believe can fulfill your expectation, then you can easily survive in the trading market.

Traders have divided trading into two parts swing trading and day trading. This book will help you to understand the difference between both the trading systems, and it will help you in choosing which trading system is best for you. The main goal of any beginner is to gain profit on their stock, whether it's a day trader or a swing trader; at the end of the day, every trader needs their name in a profit list. Even though both tradings has different tools and technical analysis procedures.

Day trading is about making multiples trades in a day. As the name suggests doing trade on your stock within a day but multiple times is day trading. This trade is all about doing trade within a day or hours. You cannot go beyond that time, and it doesn't matter how many times you trade in a day. The main objective of the day traders is to make money from their preexisting income in a day with their stock. This trade is only about day trading; it does not contain night hours. They do not keep any overnight securities. The biggest advantage of day trading is that the trader has fewer chances of having any kind of loss. For example, if a trader invests their money on any stock and the market rate of that stock goes down in the middle of the night, so in that case, the trader has to face a loss, but because of day trading, the chances of losses are also less as they will not invest their money for overnight.

According to the U.S Securities and Exchange Commission (SEC), "The Day traders typically suffer financial losses in their first months of trading, and many never graduate to profit-making status." After the SEC cautions the day trader, it was easy to understand that the beginner's traders should not take a risk by investing money more than they can afford, they should not go beyond their limitations. Most of the people commit suicide when they face loss because they had borrowed money from their friends and family or from other sources.

The day traders do not need any partner, they usually work alone, and they do not have their flexible schedule, and they do their work according to their mood and needs. They usually work at their places and take off and rap all of their stuff whenever they want. They do not need anyone's instruction because they do their work independently.

Sometimes it becomes difficult for the beginners of day traders to compete in the market because except making money and position in the market they also have to compete with the high-frequency traders, whereas other faces more advantages than the beginners as they become professionals in their work and have more experience than them. Once you start getting profit on your stock, there will be no come back from this earning adventure; you will desire to invest more and earn more.

The day trader has to generate a lot of effort and use his skills to maintain the position in the market. A beginner who wants to have all the luxuries firstly had to quit his job to maintain all his focus on trading because it would not be easy for a day trader to continue his job as it all depends on you to keep check and balance in the market. Because day trading is stressful, and the trader has to keep his self-up-to date with the ongoing situation in the market. He should be aware of multiple screening so it will help him to spot the trading opportunities.

For example

If someone is continuous his job with day trading and on the opposite hand the shares of an organization like Walmart (WMT) or Apple (AAPL) within the forex market are going high, and there's an excellent opportunity for him to trade his currency like euro or U.S. dollar (EUR/USD), so he will miss the prospect due to his job routine.

So it will be better for the future of the trader to just focus on one thing at a time, his job or a business. For trading, there are various markets; the ups and downs in the market make easier for those who cannot afford it. Once the stocks go down, buyers borrow them and sell them when the rate goes high. In the forex market, it is easier for beginners to invest their money as it requires the least capital for trading purposes. You can start from a little amount like $50, but if you can invest a large amount so it will be more useful. To gain a good position in the market, stocks trade requires to be at least $25,000 to make day trade. Day trade stock requires more capital for the better position, but if you do not have $25,000 or can't maintain your account above $25,000 then stocks are not the right place for you to invest money or do not waste your time on it, but if you have crossed $25,000, then stocks are viable day trading market. Long-time day traders love the joys of pitting their wits against the market and other professionals day in and time out. The adrenaline rush from rapid-fire trading are a few things not many traders will admit to, but it's a giant think about their decision to create a living from day trading. It's doubtful these styles of people would be content spending their days selling widgets or perusing numbers in an office cubicle.

Day trading and swing trading each have advantages and downsides. Neither strategy is healthier than the opposite, and traders should choose the approach that works best for his or her skills, preferences, and lifestyle. Day trading is healthier suited to individuals who are smitten by trading full time and possess the three Ds: decisiveness, discipline, and diligence (prerequisites for successful day trading). Swing trading, on the opposite hand, doesn't require such a formidable set of traits. Since swing trading will be undertaken by anyone with some investment capital and doesn't require full-time attention, it's a viable option for traders who want to stay their full-time jobs, but also dabble within the markets. Swing traders should even be able to apply a mixture of fundamental and technical analysis, instead of technical analysis alone.

If we differentiate swing and day trading, then they both are far different from each other, their framing time to trade is different. Swing trading is about selling and buying stock for days and weeks. Swing traders have more time to trade then the day traders. Their trading frame is longer than then day traders as they hold a position overnight. Because of their 24 hours of trading, they cannot avoid the risk that can cause a big problem against them. There will be more chances of losing money in this trade. They have to worry about the stock all the time because it could be different while opening, or it could be different from how it closed before the day. Swing traders need a lot of patience because he had to face many problems. Trades generally need time to figure out. Keeping a trade for an asset open for some days or weeks may lead to higher profits than trading in and out of the identical security multiple times daily. Swing traders know that it will take a long time, but they generally do not make it look like a full-time job. Swing trade may take a few days or maybe a few weeks to work out. Swing traders do not make this trading a full-time job career like day traders. If you have enough knowledge about swing trading and investment capital that you can try swing trading. If you are a beginner in trading and want to invest your money, then swing trading is a perfect choice because it does not require your 24/7 hours' attention, or you do not need to glued yourselves in front of your computers and keeping your eyes and fingers crossed all the time. A swing trader can even do a full-time job if he wants to because swing trading doesn't require checking on the screens all the time. The margin requirements in swing trading are higher, and usually, its maximum leverage is two times one's capital, whereas day trading has four times and one's capitals. It doesn't need constant monitoring like day trading; it can be stopped anytime whenever you feel like there is a risk in executing the trading process.

Like any other trading swing trading can also result in substantial losses. Infect swing traders has to face a larger loss than day traders as swing traders hold their position in the market for a longer time. That's why they run the risk of larger loss than day trading. Swing traders usually do have their regular jobs, and they also have other sources of income from where they can overcome theirs loses. There are more chances of burnout for swing traders due to stress in swing trading since it's seldom a full-time job. Swing traders have more chances through which they can mitigate or offset their losses.

Swing trading can be done by having just one computer, and with conventional trading tools unlike, day trading it does not require the art technology. Swing traders have overnight leverage of 50% as compared to day trading, but this margin can be risky too, particularly if margin calls occur. These trading are not so much about what you want to trade, be it commodities, i.e., oil futures or stock from the CAC 40. Instead of that, it is simply all about timing. So, where it took 4 hours and daily charts of day trading, it will be more concerned about swing trading where it took multi-day charts and candlestick patterns. Moving average crossovers, Head and shoulders patterns, shooting stars, etc. are some of the most popular.

Swing trading can be extremely challenging in two markets, the bear market environment or raging bull market. Here you will see even highly active traders will not display in the same position there will be same up and down oscillation. To invest in the stock market, it's compulsory to have a well-organized method for trading. It is very important to keep things simple, as in the early stages, it will look a bit difficult for the beginners, but instead of getting panic, they should handle them with confidence. Once you learn the rules of swing trading and the discipline, you will make money in a great quantity in the stock market. Swing trading allows you to trade in every situation, whether it is bullish, bearish, or just going sideways. This is another reason why this trade has a distinct advantage over other approaches to invest in a swing trade.

Swing traders use technical analysis indicators to identify the price swings in the market and determine the condition of the market, whether a stock price will drop or rise in the short run. Through this, they invest the capitalize in securities that have momentum and select the best time for buying or selling the stock. These technical analysis indicators help the traders to use the swing charts for their swing trading on the security current situation trend. To analyze the current trading pattern, swing traders use swing trading charts, which help the trader in providing data based on statistical analysis. Unlike day trading, swing trading is not about the long term value of the security; instead of that, they are just concerned about the ups and downs in the stock price. Swing traders can make large returns on the stock that decay in value over time because they are making returns on each small price swing of their stock while the overall trend is downward.

Swing trading and day trading appears similar in some aspects of trading. The main factor of trading is setting the two techniques apart and maintaining the position on time in the market. Unlike day traders, it does not close within minutes or in hours, it takes several weeks and overnight days. They are subjected to the unpredictability of overnight risks that may result in significant price momentum. Swing traders can check their positions in the market periodically and can take action when critical points are reached.

Main differences between swing trading and day trading are:

Trading times:

Both of them have different timings of trading. In day trading, it takes a maximum of two to four hours daily for trading purposes, and in this time, the trader manages to analyze the charts, entering and getting out of the positions, and review different stocks. Whereas the swing trader's minimum needs 45 minutes in a day, update his order and find the new one. Day trading demands more time than swing trading.

Risks:

Day trader experiences more losses than swing traders because day traders may need to carry out six trades per day, whereas swing traders may need to carry out six trades per month to maintain a good position in the market. That's why day traders had to face more struggle in maintaining their position in the market as their risk level is higher than swing traders, and they had to engage their selves more in the market then swing traders.

Stress:

Day traders are more in stress as they have to keep their selves engage all the time with the market situation. They need great knowledge about market movements and had a great level of patience. A day trader needs to be more focused on their work. On the other hand, swing traders do not take that much pressure and can't say that they are much focused than day traders.

2. HOW DOES IT WORK?

What is swing trading?

"Swing trading is a technique used for buying and selling stocks."

How does it work?

Swing trading is one of the most used and common trading strategies used in almost every market, including forex, futures trading, stocks, and much more. Swing trading is about buying and selling the stock, buying it from the market, and selling it for gains. For this purpose, traders mostly rely on technical analysis to spot good selling and buying opportunities.

Subsequently, swing trading mostly relays on fundamental assets since its great determent of significant price movements. Sometimes it will take days and even weeks. It also helps to improve trade analysis. Therefore, a trader can verify where the fundamental assets are favorable or not, or it could potentially improve instead of relying on the bearish patterns. Swing traders use the technical analysis indicator to identify the price of swing trade and determine whether a stock price will rise in the market or drop. By experiencing technical indicators, swing traders are not concerned about the long term value of the stock.

How to make swing trade with trends?

Swing trading is one of the best solid tradings, and it has one of the obvious trends in trading strategies. For beginners, it is necessary to understand its importance in the market that once you get to know how to invest your money, it will offer a lot of high possibility of trading opportunities with a high upside. For a beginner, it is obligatory to have enough knowledge about the market. The initial step that every beginner should take is to identify the market needs, he should know about the market trends.

For getting a good position in the market, every trader should go with the best trends, any trend that goes on the top of the list that if you show them to a child, they would clearly choose the right one whose prices are getting higher or lower.

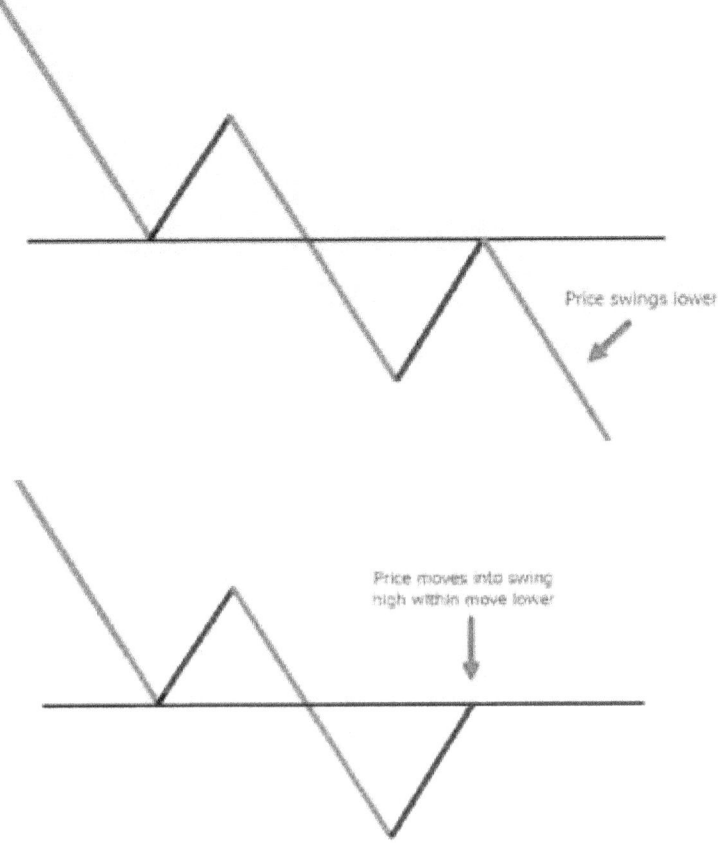

One of the most common mistakes that every beginner makes when looking to swing trade within a trend is not entering with the right swing point.

Tips for Beginners

When you should choose Swing trading:

Swing trading is easier than day trading, but to see whether choosing swing trading is a good decision for you or not, you should enlist all the points and see which one will give you more profit.

- Make sure that you are ready to spend your days, weeks, and months on this trading as swing trading contains a longer period for trading.

- If you already have a job and want to invest your money for extra income, but you do not have enough time to sit in front of a computer, then swing trading is the best option for you.

- You do not need to do constant monitoring and keeping an eye on market activities.

- Swing trading will give you a less stressful life and will reduce the risk level.

- As a beginner, you should always have a plan and stick to it as it's the nature of buying and selling that there will be highs and lows, but you should stick to the plan.

- Before you start swing trading, you should practice it by watching markets. Having knowledge about pre-trading will help you in gaining the loss.

- Don't expect to have money on a quick note; just focus on your aim and let the process sink in.

- Having a good observation will help you in investing money in the right stock, so if you want to gain money on the first stock, then you should know how to use the technical analysis indicators.

- It is important for a beginner to keep in mind while trading the entrance and exit strategy. Before entering a market, we should check everything and keep ourselves update with the study of the charts, noting the price the stock will likely reach in its current swing.

- Most of the traders (like partygoers) find it more favorable to choose how to exit before they have entered the trade.

- There will be more chances of losing money in the earlier stages of trading, but a good trader should stick to it and should gather basic skills, polish those skills, learn new technical techniques, and improve your knowledge. It's important not to give up in a condition.

- He should read books and follow the swing trading tips for beginners.

Trading Platforms

For successful swing trading, the trader should select the right stocks to make a profit in the market. Therefore, traders can also opt for stock with large market capitalization. The most active assets will be among beginners, and they will be the most actively traded ones on top exchange. If we talk about the platforms for swing trading, then, on the one hand, there is a bear market, and on the other is the bull market. Similarly, there is a stable market between both of them. Yet swing trading in a bear or bull market is pretty different from that stable one.

For example, stocks in the market might tend to spike and dump using various patterns in both of these markets, unlike a stable market where a similar pattern could have upheld for weeks or months. In the bear market and bull market, the momentum can cause stocks to trade in a specific way for a long time. In that situation, to gain the maximum profit, a trader should trade in the way of the long term trend. And to experience that profit, a swing trader has to correctly regulate the current market, whether it is bearish or bullish.

The simple moving average (SMA) recommends specific support and resistance stages. It also displays bullish and bearish patterns. When the stock knockouts the support level, it signals a virtuous time to purchase, and once it hits the resistance level, then it's a good time to trade. The bullish and bearish methods also signal entry and exit price points. Therefore, another form of SMA is the exponential moving average (EMA), and it focuses on state-of-the-art data points. The trend signals, as well as entry or exit points presented by the EMA, is quicker compared to the SMA. The 9, 13, and 50 periods EMA can be used to improved time entry points.

For example, when the price of a stock crosses these EMAs, it shows a bullish trend. Therefore, there could probably be a problem with the bearish trend. For instance, when the 9 EMA crosses the 13 EMA, whereas the 13 EMA is above the 50-period EMA, it signals a buying opportunity.

What is day trading?

"Selling and buying a stock multi times in a day."

How does day trading work?

It seems very interesting to trade, and those who wanted to join this trading system may see it with more interest because it seems very easy and interesting, but in reality, the life of a trader is like living a life on the edge. In day trading, we don't have any idea what will happen in the very next moment; unexpected event scan occur at any time. The bitter reality of trading is that most of the days are dry and are quite ordinary, and at the very next moment, you will see your name at the top of the list. In day trading, the high speed of execution is very important as you may see the high numbers of trades you could make in a day to match yourself with the market price you need to match the level of the market. To make your trading work, it is very important to lower the commission rates. It will be more viable day trading as it will have a lower fee rate. Beginners should keep regulatory compliance in their trading. Day traders usually start off with zero positions in their typical portfolios, and day traders trade so frequently that by the end of the day, they have closed all of their trades.

Some day traders work manually, making trade by trade hour by the hour using a chart. Others set up an automatic process that makes orders to purchase and trade for them. Whereas day traders don't actually look at fundamental data, they are concerned in price volatility, liquidity, breaking trends, and trading volume of the day that will change a stock price significantly.

REMINDER:

For day trading, forex is the best platform. For practicing forex and futures trading, a trader should use the Ninja Trader Replay feature. It will help in practicing historical trade days as if you are trading for real.

How to make day trade with trends?

It's very necessary for a trader to follow the market trends for getting a strong position in a market. Trading against the trend and not following it is one of the most common reasons for facing failure in trading. Poor quality of trend and not following a trend is a major reason for not getting the buyer's attention. Those who follow quality and strong trends have more chances of gaining success in trading. In trading, the trend raises the over-all direction of a stock's price. There is another possibility of having traders who are not mentally and physically active all the time to respond to a large number of stocks or price changes. For those who cannot manage things by themselves, they can use a stock screener; it will help the trader to narrow down the number of stocks and decrease the size so that it will make things easier in working for you. If you follow the trending tactics, only trade stocks that have a trending tendency. If you have a stock screener or an assistant, then they can help you isolating stocks that trend so that you will be having a list of stocks, and you can easily apply your day trading strategies through it. Whatever stock you choose to trade represents your trading style, and a good trading style always held a good position in the market.

For stocks, the finest time for day trading is the first one to two hours after the opening, and the last hour before the closing of the market. 9:30 a.m. to 11:30 a.m. The chances of good day trading opportunities usually start a bit earlier than others in the stock market. The forex market trades 24-hours a day throughout the week. The EURUSD is the famous day trading pair. This currency pair usually records better trading volumes between 1 A.M. and 12 P.M. EST. London markets are opened during these hours. Day traders would trade within these hours. The hours from 7 A.M. to 10 A.M. EST typically generate the biggest price changes because both the London and New York markets are opened during this duration. Therefore, this is a very common and active time for day traders.

Tips for Beginners

When you should choose day trading:

For a beginner, it is very important to make a list of all those things that can help him in becoming a good trader and list all those negative points too that can create a problem. Choosing the correct time for trading is very important when you are mentally and physically ready to devote yourself to this path.

- Firstly, see whether you are fulfilling all the requirements of SEC and FINRA pattern day trader rule.

- Give yourself a minute and think that whether you are ready to sit in front of a computer for two to four hours continuously for keeping yourself update from the current situation of the market.

- You need a lot of patience to become a good trader; that's why it is very important to keep your patience level up.

- A trader does not need a college degree or professional degree for day trading. Neither a trader needs to learn thousands of books.

- Discipline is very important for trading; if you start violating everything, then you can never trade your stock in the market.

- A day trader should have the ability to take a risk and managing things if he faces the loss.

- He should not take stress over things but should control them in a good manner.

- You should have a computer for trading, having two monitors is preferable but not necessary. Your computer should have a great memory and fast processer as it can give you a disadvantage if the processer or software is not good.

- Having a good internet connection is another most important thing if you lose the connection during a trade than you will also lose the trade too.

- To start your trading career, it is necessary to select the right platform. As the beginners do not have enough knowledge about the right platform as you are not aware of a well-developed trading style.

- In day trading, a trader doesn't need to trade all day. You will possibly discover more stability by only trading two to three hours a day.

- Make a note about your chart of profits/losses in pips (forex), points (futures), or cents (stocks) on a daily basis because these are scalable figures. Writing down dollar figures can make you confuse because there will be more chances that your account balance may fluctuate by the time, resulting in bigger or smaller trades.

- Save all the gathered data with a name, month-day-year.
- Make a folder on your computer and store the saved files over there for later reviews.
- Each weekend, go through the gathered data from the previous week.
- Note where you made a mistake and what you need to improve in yourself.
- Day traders should practice all the precise issues in a demo account during non-trading hours.

NOTE:

For having a good position in the market, the trader should find the repeating patterns that are making continually profit in the market.

Trading Platforms

A beginner always has the trading platform in his mind whenever he thinks to start trading where he should trade or not, which platform will be more beneficial for him. The future of trade is more often based on the indexes and commodities. A beginner could trade gold, crude oil, or S&P movements. Not every market is good; it changes and comes down to what you trade and what you can afford by the time. There are a lot of markets for trading that can help beginners in achieving their goals, but finding the right one to invest your money is very important. Day traders are admirable risk-takers. They take risks in that area where they can't afford to take risks. Still, they utilize this trading platform. Day traders must have a fast, reliable platform full of tools and features to ensure an optimal trading experience.

There are thousands of stocks in the market to choose, how do you decide which one will give you more profit or you are going to focus on for day trading? It can be confusing for a beginner trying to figure out the right one. Some day traders find easily new stocks to trade every day or hunt for stocks that are breaking out of patterns. Therefore, others lookout for stocks that breakout of support or resistance levels or are the most volatile. A beginner should keep these things in his mind while choosing a market, that when you have picked up a market for your investment, you should have the proper equipment and software setup, and knowledge about the goods for day trading. When you start thinking about trading, you need to know how to control risk. Day traders may control risk in two ways: trade risk and daily risk. Trade risk is how far you are willing to take the risk on each trade. Ideally, about risk 1% or less of your money on each trade.

A beginner can also start his trade with a little amount of $50, although if he can invest more than starting with more is recommended. Whereas some trading markets required $1,000 to get started. A day trader at least requires $25,000 to trade for his stock. The need for having more capitals to day trade stock will not make it better or worse in the market than the others. It is essential for trading to maintain your position good in the market for that you have to maintain your account up to $25,000, but if you are facing continual failure, then this market is not a good place for you.

3. SWING TRADING AND DAY TRADING: TACTICS AND STRATEGIES

What is strategy?

"Strategy is an action or plan that is used to attain one or more of the organizational aims."

A trading strategy is a procedure through which a trader sells and buys the stock and is based on predefined rules used to make trading decisions. Any type of trading process in the market usually includes a well-considered trading and investing plan that specifies risk tolerance, tax implication, and capitalizing objects. Applying or planning a strategy in trading means that a trader should search and adopt the best practices and ideas and then follows them.

REMINDER:

The strategy includes three stages: Planning a trade, placing a trade, and then executing it.

A trader should understand the level of risk he can take and then decide what is appropriate for him to do. Trading strategies are mainly based on either fundamentals or methodological. To avoid behavioral finance biases and to make sure about consistent results, trading strategies are employed. Even though it is very difficult to develop a trading strategy because there are more chances of having a risk of becoming over-reliant on a strategy.

How many strategies does a trader need?

A trader should use only one or two strategies for successful trading. It is a pattern of buying and selling the stocks every trader uses in their daily routine, which outlines when a trader will enter and exit the market. The trading strategy allows the trader to see the trading opportunities objectively. It also allows the trader to see how the trades and traders have worked out in the past.

Types of strategies:

There are four types of trading styles.

1. Scalping.
2. Day trading.
3. Position trading.
4. Swing trading.

Trading styles, time frame and their time of a period frame are given below:

Trading Style	Time Frame	Time Period of Frame
Scalping	Short-term	Seconds or minutes
Day trading	Short-term	For one day (maximum)

Position trading	Long-term	Weeks, months, or years.
Swing Trading	Medium-term	Days or weeks

These trading styles are the four main types of trading mostly use in the forex market.

Day trading strategy

Day trading strategies are important for the trader when he is looking to capitalize on small price movements. A trading strategy helps the trader to understand how from thousands of stocks, a reader can decide or choose the right one. This book will help beginners to understand the market situation and helps in focusing on which strategy will help the trader. Sometimes beginners get confused due to their zero experience in the beginning, and they lose their hopes, but here we will try to end the confusion of the trading beginners before it actually begins in their minds. A consistent, effective strategy in day trading relies on utilizing charts, technical indicators, in-depth technical analysis, and patterns; it helps in predicting future price movements in trading. This book will give you a detailed breakdown of beginners' trading strategies. The fast step of moving investment positions in a single trading day creates a perception that day trading is riskier or extra volatile than other types of trading.

It is essential for a beginner to know the basic concept of trading because it could bog down a trader in a complex world of highly technical indicators, that's why focus and knowledge both are important for a simple day trading strategy. Having patience and control is very important for the day trader because there will be days when it will turn out to be ranging days in trading. One of the most common mistakes that every beginner usually makes is taking the risk of trading too early while knowing it can damage them financially, still trying to get a better price and position in the market and assuming that the trade will trigger them in the future. This is the biggest mistake that every beginner has usually made.

Basic strategic fundamentals every day trader should use:

- A trader should not expect to make a fortune if he is only allocating an hour or two a day to trading. A trader needs to continuously monitor the markets and keep looking for trading chances.
- Before you start doing trading, first, you need to decide how much you're prepared to take a risk. A trader should keep in mind that most successful traders won't put more than 2% of their investment on the line per trade.
- A trader should prepare himself for some losses if he wants to be around when the winner's start rolling in.
- A trader should make sure that he should stay up to date with the events and market news that will influence your asset, such as a shift in economic policy. A trader can discover a wealth of online economic and business resources that will keep them in the know.

- For trading, just having the knowledge of the market intricacies isn't enough; a trader should be informed about everything.

- The trading market will get volatile when it opens each day and while practiced day traders who are capable of reading the outlines and profit, a trader should bide his time

- It's tougher than it looks to keep your emotions at bay when you are five coffees in, and you have been watching at the screen for hours. A trader should let maths, logic, and the trading strategy guide him rather than nerves, fear, or greed.

- A trader must have technical tools in the beginning, but also the best place to experiment with new strategies for advanced traders is the demo account. Several demo accounts are unrestricted, so not time restriction.

Important Components for day trading:

Whether it is automated day trading strategies, or advanced tactics and beginner, a trader will need to take three essential components; liquidity, volatility, and volume. If a beginner wants to create money by making tiny price movements, choosing the right stock is vigorous. These three elements will help the trader to make a decision.

1. Liquidity:

This enables the trader to suddenly enter and exit trades at an eye-catching and stable price. Liquid commodity strategies, for example, crude oil, focus on gold, and natural gas, etc.

2. **Volatility:**

Through this, every beginner trader will get to know about their potential profit range. The larger the volatility, the larger profit or loss a trader may make. The cryptocurrency market is an example of high volatility.

3. **Volume:**

This measurement will help the beginner to know about how many times the stock/asset has been traded within a set period of time. For a day trader beginners, this is known as 'average daily trading volume.' High volume helps in knowing that there's significant interest in the asset or security. Growth in volume is often an indicator a price goes either up or down, is fast approaching.

How much risk is involved in day trading?

According to the experts of (OTA) Online Trading Academy, it is a reality that day trading situations managing in a single day are making it truly safer rather than riskier.

"One of the best ways to control risk is limiting the length of the trade. The longer you are in a position, the greater the likelihood is that price could move against you. By day trading, you eliminate overnight and weekend risk, especially when you trade markets that close, like stocks."

– Brandon Wendell, CMT

Because it is a fact that day traders don't hold their positions overnight, they usually avoid the probability of a surprise in an overseas market, unfavorable financial news, or an incomes report that comes out once the markets are closed. Even though after-hours trading is offered for numerous securities, the market is high, and it's possible that the position will *gap down* and open at a dramatically lower price the next day after a negative overnight experience.

In addition, day trading tends to give ease, not increase market volatility. Day traders are usually looking for their earnings in small price movements up or down. Their daily trades offer liquidity, which helps the marketing the running easily, as compared to casually traded markets that are subject to dramatic price swings. Day trading is not a way to become rich instantly. Day trading is a traditional investing approach that is used by many organizations as well by the well-educated institutions who have adopted it as a profession.

In the 1990s, day trading did not have a good reputation, and at that time, many beginners began day trading. They started jumping into different platforms, including online trading platforms, without applying the stock strategies. They believed that they could run the market without having the knowledge about the market and make a fortune in stock trades with their little effort. This proved them wrong.

What do you need to start day trading?

For a day trader beginner, it is important to have technical equipment at your place. Most of the beginners think that daily trading requires heavy and expensive equipment and high investments of capital; that's not the reality.

Here's a list of items usually every trader needs for trading.

Technology:

For trading, traders do not want a supercharged computer with a dozen monitors to trade. They only need one laptop or a computer.

Internet Connection:

It is very important to have a good internet connection; it helps the trader to process his order in a timely manner. Most cables and even satellites suppliers offer sufficient bandwidth to connect to the exchanges. Typical packages of 20mbps of cable internet are enough for this. Most of the traders even use their mobile phone connections of 5mbps to 20mbps, but that is not suggested. The slow mobile phone connection can cause delays in transactions and can cause unexpected loss.

Trading Platform:

Traders should be careful in the trading market because there are many online brokers sitting online to fool the beginners. They offer the beginners their services but route orders over market makers who cost additional money, they often deferral the processing. It is easy to perform trade analysis and place your orders very quickly and properly. The web-based version is less reliable then the downloaded version, the downloaded version offers more features.

Skills

Lots of people are supporters of seeking an education. The main problem is that; education alone is not enough unless it is being utilized rightly in the market. Although having information about the markets, how it will work, and how to read price is essential, and how it will offer an advantage, skill is also necessary to obtain stable results.

Building a skill involves practice and experience, but trying to get trading skills without supervision can be a lengthy, often annoying process. For many traders, working and learning from the experience of a counselor is the best way to improve any of the skills and learn strategies for trading and investing that reduces risk. Even the famous traders like Paul Tudor and Warren Buffett Jones needed mentors. Mr. Buffett worked under Benjamin Graham, and Mr. Jones worked under Eli Tullis.

Day Trading Strategies

Strategies

1. Breakout

In trading breakout strategies center around after the price clears a specified level on the chart, with improved volume. The breakout trader enters into a long situation once the security or asset breaks above resistance. Otherwise, a trader enters a short site after the stock breaks below support.

Once a security or asset trades beyond the quantified amount barrier, volatility frequently increases, and the amount will often trend in the way of the breakout.

A trader needs to catch the right instrument to trade. While doing this, bear in the notice the resistance level and asset's support. The more often the price has hit these facts, the more authenticated and vital they become.

Plan the Entry and Exits Points:

This part of trading is good and direct. Prices set to nearby and above resistance levels want a bearish place. Prices set to nearby and below a maintenance level want a bullish place.

Using the asset's latest performance to establish a sensible price target. Using chart patterns in trading will make this process even more precise. A trader can analyze the average current price swings to generate a target. If the average swings have been 3 points over the last some price swings, this would be a workable target. Once you've got hold of that goal, then you can exit the trade and enjoy the profit.

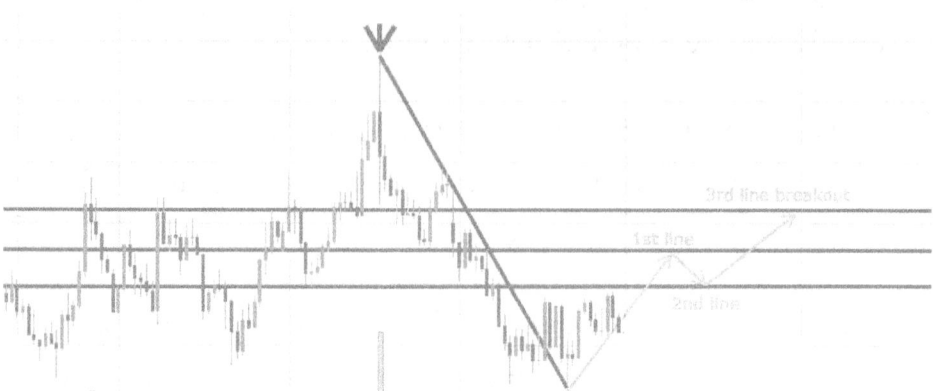

2. Scalping

Scalping is one of the best strategies, mostly used by traders. It is mostly used, and it is popular in the forex market. It looks to capitalize on minute price changes, and its driving force is quantity. You will look to sell the stock as soon as the stock becomes profitable. This is an exciting and fast-paced technique to trade, but then again, it can be risky. You must have a high trading probability to even out the reward ratio vs. low risk. A trader should be on the lookout for volatile tools, attractive liquidity, and be on timing. You cannot wait for the market; you must close losing trades as soon as possible.

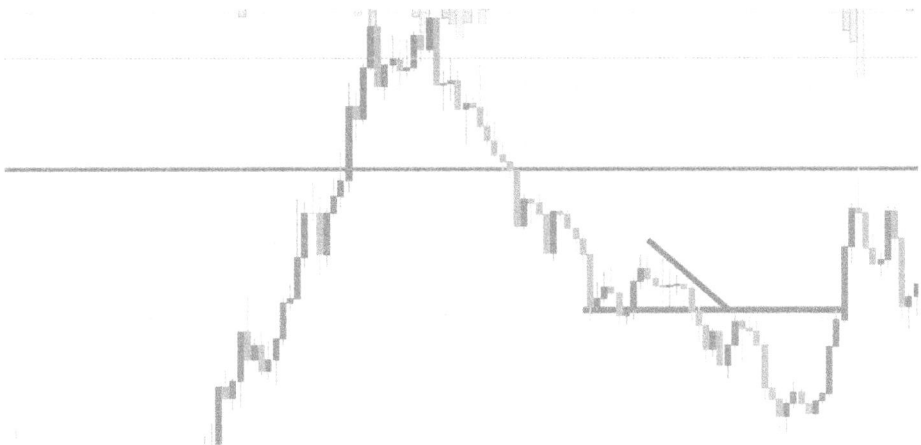

3. Momentum:

This strategy is popular among all trading strategies for beginners; this strategy revolves around acting on recognizing large trending moves with the support of high volume and news sources. For the ample opportunity, there is always at least one stock that moves around 20-30% each day. A trader simply holds onto the position until he sees signs of reversal and then gets out. Otherwise, he can disappear the price drop. This way round his price target as soon as volume starts to shrink.

This is the simplest and most effective strategy if used properly. However, a trader must ensure that he is aware of upcoming news and income announcements. Just a small number of seconds on each trade will make all the difference to your end of day profits.

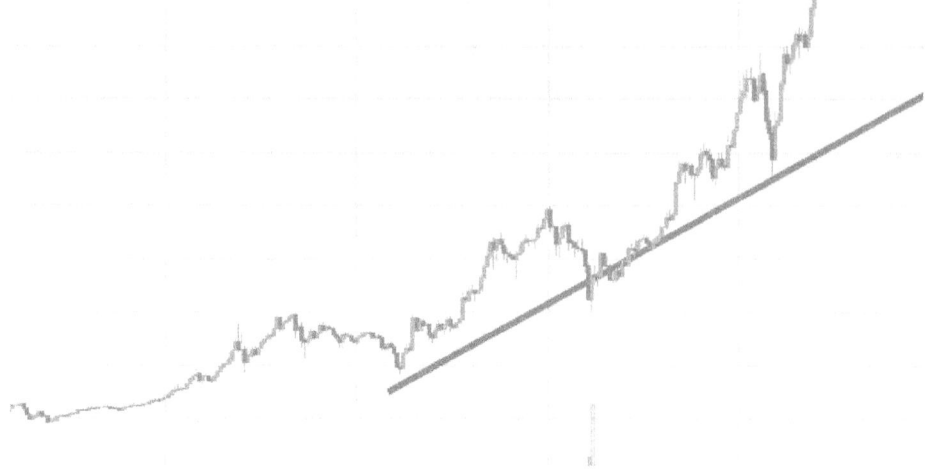

4. Reversal

Though this strategy is hotly debated and potentially unsafe when it comes to using by beginners. Reverse trading is used all over the world. It's also known as pullback trending, trend trading, and a mean reversion strategy. This strategy confronts the basic logic as the trader aims to trade against the trend. A trader must be able to correctly classify possible pullbacks, plus calculate their strength. To do this effectively, a trader must need in-depth market experience and knowledge.

The 'daily pivot' strategy is measured as a unique case of reverse trading, as it centers on selling and buying the daily high and low pullbacks/reverse.

5. Using Pivot Points

A day trading pivot point strategy can be strange or fantastic in trading for acting on critical support and/or resistance levels identifying it. It is mostly useful in the forex market. In addition, pivot points can be used by range-bound traders to recognize points of entry, whereas trend and breakout traders can use pivot points to locate key levels that must break a move to count as a breakout.

Calculating Pivot Points

A pivot point is well-defined as a point of rotation in day trading. A beginner day trader can use the prices of the previous day's low or high and, plus the closing price of a security to analyze the pivot point.

Note that if you analyze a pivot point using price statistics from a quite short time frame, accuracy is often reduced.

So, how does a day trader will analyze/calculate the pivot point?

- Central Pivot Point (P) = (High + Low + Close) / 3

Now day traders can analyze resistance and support levels by using the pivot point. For doing that a trader must use the following formulas:

- First Resistance (R1) = (2*P) – Low
- First Support (S1) = (2*P) – High

The second level of resistance and support is then calculated as follows:

- Second Resistance (R2) = P + (R1-S1)
- Second Support (S2) = P – (R1- S1)

Application

When practically applied in the FX market, for example, a beginner will find the trading range for the session that will frequently take place among the pivot point and the resistance levels and the first support. The reason behind this is having a high number of traders playing this range. It is also worth noting because this is one of the systems &approaches that can be applied to indexes too.

For example, it can help a day trader beginner to form an effective S&P day trading strategy.

Limit Your Losses

This is the most important thing to keep in your mind if you are using a margin is limiting your loss. Requirements are often high for day traders. When a day trader trades on a margin, he will be increasingly susceptible to sharp price movements. This means the potential for a bigger profit, but it also means the probability of substantial losses. Luckily, a trader can employ stop-losses. The stop-loss controls the trade risk for the trader. In a small situation, a trader can place a stop-loss above a recent high; for good big situations, you can place it below a recent low. A trader can also make it dependent on volatility.

For example, if a stock amount moves by £0.05 a minute, so you can place a stop-loss £0.15 away after your entry order, letting it swing (hopefully in the expected direction).

One popular strategy in day trading is to set up two stop-losses. Firstly, a trader places a physical stop-loss order at a precise price level. This will be the maximum capital you can afford to lose. Secondly, you can create a mental stop-loss. Place this, at the point of your entry criteria, are breached. So if the trade makes an unexpected turn, you'll make a swift exit.

Forex Trading Strategies

Forex strategies are risky by nature as a trader must accumulate his profits in a short space of time. A trader can apply any of the strategies in the forex market.

Swing trading strategy

What is a swing trader?

Swing traders are basically those traders that trade for a couple of days or for weeks' time frame. They usually work for four hours (H4) and daily (D1) charts, and they may use a blend of fundamental analysis and technical analysis to monitor trading their decisions. Whether it is a long term trend or whether the market is mainly range-bound, it really does not matter. A Forex swing trader is not going to hold on to a position that is enough for it to count considerably.

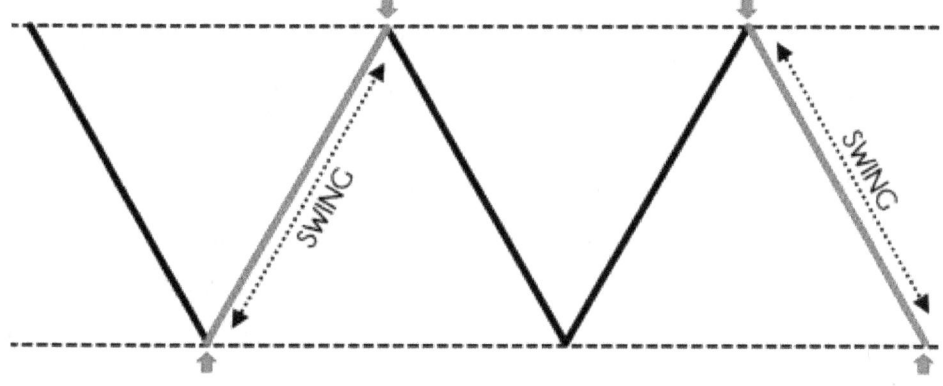

In the trading market, the swing trader is best to be used when markets are going nowhere once indexes rise for multi-days, then decay for the next few days, only to repeat the same over-all patterns again and again. Swing trader has several chances to catch the short-term movements up and down. The problem with swing trading and long-term trend trading is that success is established on correctly recognizing what type of market is presently being practiced. Trend trading might have the perfect strategy for the bull market of the 1990s, while swing trading maybe would have been best for 2000 and 2001.

Simple moving averages (SMAs) offer resistance and support levels, as well as bearish and bullish patterns. Support and resistance levels can help the trader in buying a stock. Bullish and bearish limit patterns signal price ideas where you should enter and exit stocks. The exponential moving average (EMA) is similar to SMA that places extra emphasis on the latest data points. The EMA gives traders clear trend indications, entry, and exit points faster than a simple moving average (SMA). Swing trades can use EMA for entry and exit points.

A swing trader tends to look for multi-day chart outlines. Some of the more common outlines include moving average crossovers, head and shoulders patterns, flags, triangles, and cup-and-handle patterns. Eventually, each swing trader formulates a plan and strategy that gives them an advantage over many trades. This also includes looking for trade arrangements that tend to lead to expectable movements in the asset's price. This is not that easy, and no strategy or any arrangement will work every time. Through a favorable risk or reward, winning every time is not required. The more promising risk or reward of a trading strategy, the fewer times it desires to win in order to produce a complete profit over many trades.

Once it comes to take profits, the swing traders, whether they are beginners or the professionals, they will want to exit the trade as soon as possible to the upper or lower channel line without being too defined, which can cause the risk of missing the finest opportunity.

In the book of Dr. Alexander Elder, "Come Into My Trading Room: A Complete Guide to Trading" (2002), he uses his understanding of a stock's behavior above and below the baseline to define the swing trader's strategy of "buying regularity and selling mania" or "shorting regularity and covering depression." Once the swing trader used the EMA to recognize the typical baseline on the stock chart, the trader goes long at the baseline once the stock is heading up and short at the baseline once the stock is on its way down.

Therefore, swing traders are not looking to smash the home run by a single trade; they are not alarmed with the perfect time to purchase a stock exactly at its bottom and sell exactly at its top. In a perfect trading environment, beginners should wait for the stock to hit its baseline and confirm its way before they make their moves. The story becomes more complex when a tougher uptrend or downtrend is at play. The trader may unexpectedly go long once the stock dips below its EMA and pause for the stock to go back up in an uptrend, or a trader may short a stock that has stuck above the EMA and wait for it to drop if the time-consuming trend is down.

NOTE:

Many traders believe that they cannot make trades by greater as their account is too small.

If a trader is calculating his position before each trade and risking a similar amount in each trade, then a trader ought to be able to play a trade whether the stop is 60 pips or 10.

Popular Swing Trading Strategies:

Swing trading is frequently done within trends, and this is a common way; it can also be successfully carried out in ranging markets. A swing trader analyses the price profit and action from the greater part of the market's next swing. The markets spend far-off extra of their time reaching; then they do create clear trends higher or lower and being capable to successfully trade ranging markets, is critical.

Forex Swing Trading Strategies:

Swing trading is not a strategy; it is a style. The time frame of swing trading describes this style, and within that, there are unlimited strategies that we can use to swing trade. Swing trading is a style that works over short to moderate time frames. Swing trading style lies between the very long time frames of position trading and short time frames of day trading. It is not so short that it requires all your time observing the market, yet it is short enough to offer plenty of trading chances. These strategies are not limited to swing trading; it is the case with most technical strategies, support and resistance are the ideas behind them.

These concepts can give a trader two choices within the swing trading strategy with, following the trend, or trading counter to the trend. Counter trending strategies aim to profit once support and resistance levels hold up. Trend following strategies looks for the chances when support and resistance levels break down.

For trading swing traders can use the following strategies for actionable trading opportunities:

Swing trading strategy 1: Trend trading

When classifying a trend, it's essential to recognize that markets don't tend to move in a straight line. Even while eventually trending, they move up and down in step like moves. A trader should recognize an uptrend by the market, making higher highs and higher lows, and a downtrend by recognizing lower lows and lower highs. Many swing trading strategies of trying to catch and follow a short trend.

Swing trading strategy 2: Counter-trend trading

The next swing trading strategy is counter-trend trading and therefore does the reverse of the first one. We practice the similar principles in terms of trying to spot relatively short-term trends from building, but now try to profit as of the frequency with which these trends tend to break down.

NOTE:

Uptrend = Higher lows and Higher highs

Downtrend = Lower lows and lower highs

A counter-trend trader would effort to catch the swing in this period of reversion. Therefore, the trader would try to identify the break in the trend. In an uptrend, this might be a fresh high was followed by a series of failures to break new highs. Hence we go short in expectation of such a reversion. The reverse is true in a downtrend.

Itis very important to maintain a strong discipline encounter trending if the price travels against you, and if the market resumes its trend against you, then you should be ready to admit that you are wrong, and you had drawn a line under the trade.

Swing trading strategy 3: A versatile swing trading strategy

If a trader would like to take an even deeper dive into swing trading, besides learning a multipurpose strategy that even beginners can use. Being a versatile trader means that a trader is able to trade any instrument, in any timeframe or in any direction.

Improving swing trading strategies for beginners:

What swing can traders do to increase their strategies?

There are numerous things a trader can try. The first thing is to effort to match the trade with the long-term trend. While the hourly chart helps the swing trader to also look at a longer-term chart to get a feel for the long-standing trend. Try and trade merely once your direction matches whatever you see as the long-term trend. Another way to recover your swing trading strategy is to use a technical indicator to confirm your thinking.

A moving average (MA) is one more indicator you can use to help. An MA flattens the prices to give a clearer view of the trend. And because an MA includes older price data, it's an easy way to match how the recent prices compare to older prices.

Managing risk in Forex swing trading:

Have you ever read about trading Forex and that the widely held of traders that lost money because of it? Have you ever understood that this is even true for successful traders?

The reality is that no trader wins 100% of the time. Most of the time it happens that the beginners of the swing trading misjudge the market, sometimes it moves unexpectedly, sometimes the trader might just make a mistake. This is the point where risk management and money management are so important.

In trading, but especially in Forex, a trader should know how to lose before knowing how to get success. And when traders talk about having enough knowledge on how to lose, he should also know how to lose tiny to win big. Basically, if a trader can achieve a swing trading risk, then he can close out losing trades early, which will help to ensure he enjoys extra profits than losses.

Some tips for handling your risk in swing trading include:

1. Maximum acceptable loss:

In spite of the fact that a trade clearly wants his next trade to make a profit, it's important to think through the supreme amount you are prepared to lose on a trade. The minute a trader knows this amount can set a stop loss to close his trade spontaneously if it travels too far in the incorrect direction then this will help to protect him when he can't automatically be at your computer observing every trade.

2. Taking a risk on any one trade:

No matter what is the size of your trading account, you must avoid risking your whole balance on a trade. If a trader does not follow that, then he can possibly lose it all. Andover-all rule is not to risk more than 2% of your account balance on any one trade.

3. Increasing account balance to diversify risk:

Despite the fact that a trader might be able to open an account from as little as €300, it is better to start using a larger sum. This means that a trader will have an adequate amount of your account to trade a diversity of assets and expand the risk of swing trading. Swing trading is by description a long-term investment style, so you need extra verge on your places to manage with market explosive nature.

4. Information about your profile:

One of the first and most important things to do when you start trading in the market is to understand your risk aversion and volatility. In other words, at what stage of the loss will a trader starts to panic? If a swing trader has an account balance of €25,000 and he has lost €3,000, then this means that the trader has lost 10% of his capital. In that case, would he be a failure, or would he think through that to be usual? How the trader will respond to this loss will influence the risks he is willing to take in trading.

You can see that this strategy will be easy for a beginner to understand. Therefore, a Swing Trading strategy is an average and long-term trading strategy. This strategy is very dependent on the capital and management of risks. It is most commonly called money management swing trading.

Swing trading money management:

Once a trader understands the big picture of the trading after that, he still has to manage his risk every day in the market. And one way to do trading wisely is by managing your money successfully. It might give the impression like a complex question, but in reality, it doesn't have to be.

For example: If a trader wanted to keep the total risk of 6% of his account balance so he could have six trades opened, each risking 1% of his assets.

For that reason, a trader could lose 1% of his capital in six different trades or a maximum amount of €200 in each trade if you had an account of €20,000. At that point, before taking a position, a trader should be aware of his maximum risk for proper management of his assets in Swing Trading that will be 1% or 200 euros. For that reason, your stop-loss and neutralization position will be determined previously by each position. And from there, you should perform as many actions as you can without overcoming your risk management.

That boundary will then affect your actions, and you will close since the trade is approaching your loss limit, or you will lose the trade because the asset goes up and reaches the target profit. And if a trade passes the breakeven fact, at which point it develops a 'neutral' trade, you can take on a new site, without endangering your risk limit.

The best tools for swing trading:

There is a range of tools a trader can use to improve his chances of success while performing swing trading strategies.

Some ranges that are recommended:

- **Correlation Matrix:** The relationship between Forex pairs, supplies, or stock guides is one element of analysis that allows sensible trading to trade with self-confidence.

- **Mini Charts**:

A mini charting tool permits the trader to analyze numerous units of time on a single chart. Which means that there is no need for the trader to shift from swing chart W1 to D1 to come to be on the H4 chart to discover his entry point

- **Symbol Info:**

In the same manner, this Forex swing indicator lets traders understand on a single chart the trading signals of the maximum used indicators on eight different interval scales.

- **Mini Terminal:**

The mini terminal tool allows the trader to open a place in Meta Trader in a second, but then again, it also permits the swing trader to open trades regarding the risk in permanent euros or in percentage. In fact, it provides you with diverse information associated with the stock market or the currency pair in which a trader can apply it, including the current trend, the strength of current movements and current momentum

Other useful indicators for swing traders include are:

- Exponential Mobile Average
- MACD
- Overwhelming oscillator
- Parabolic SAR
- CCI
- Admiral Donchian

So here comes the question that troubles the beginners, that from where the beginners of swing trading can access these swing trading tools? It's easy for those who have a demo or a live account with Admiral Markets. And if not, then the good news is that any of the beginners can easily access these totally free with Meta-Trader Supreme Edition.

Meta-Trader Supreme Edition is an absolutely free plugin for MT4 and MT5 that contains a range of unconventional features, such as an indicator package with technical analysis trading ideas provided by Trading Central, and 16 new indicators and mini terminals and mini charts to mark your trading even more effectual.

Top tips for Forex swing trading for beginners:

After knowing the basics of the swing, and after having enough information about the Forex swing trading strategies, here are the top tips that will help you to succeed as a swing trader.

1. Match your trades by the long-term trend:

Although a trader may always be looking at a time chart of shorter-term (e.g., H1 or H4), it may also comfort the beginner to look at a longer-term chart (D1 or W1) to get the information about the long-term trend. Then you can make sure that you aren't trading beside a larger trend. Swing trading is also much easier when it's been trading by means of the trend, rather than against the trend.

2. Make the best of Moving Averages (MAs):

The MA indicator may profit the trader to classify trends by moderating shorter-term price differences. Since the MA comprises old data prices, it is the easiest way to associate what way the existing price links with older prices.

3. Use a little leverage:

Leverage lets the trader access a larger position than it would usually let your deposit, together with strengthening your profits and losses. Once used wisely, leverage can help the trader to make the most of winning trades.

4. Trade a wide-ranging portfolio of Forex pair:

Lookout as several currency pairs as you can to discover the best opportunities. The Forex market will every time offer you trading opportunities you want; you need to look for the ones that match best with your signal. Plus, trading a range of pairs will support to diversify your portfolio, and achieve the risk of having all your eggs in one basket.

5. Pay attention to swaps:

Swaps are a cost of trading concern charge ready for positions held overnight. These swaps need to be taken into account in swing trading of the trader in order to be able to manage your money better.

6. Maintaining a positive profit/loss ratio:

Whether it is H4 or daily trading, swing trading allows the trader to tap into large market schedules, giving the trader the chance to get larger profit ratios associated with very small losses possible, especially when matched to scalping.

7. Put a side your sentiments:

It's better to trade without emotions, but then again, to make swing trades as a part of a fixed Forex trading plan and strategy.

Choose a Broker for Forex Swing:

Before a trader starts trading, a trader needs to choose a broker. Choosing a broker for the Forex market will give a chance to the new traders to access the markets in a way that wants to trade, along with a trading platform to carry out his trades. Though some brokers are better than others, that's why it is essential to keep the following in mind while making a choice.

- Check if they are synchronized by the local regulator in your area? Admiral Markets is a Forex and CFD broker that is controlled by the EFSA, ASIC CYSEC, and FCA.

- The costs of trading contain the spread, the swap, and orders on trades, which know how to eat into your profits. That's why it is essential to have knowledge about typical trading costs.

- A standard Forex share, or trading contract, is value 100,000 of the base currency of the pair before the first currency listed (if one share of the EUR/USD costs EUR 100,000). For new traders, this might be extra than you want to see, so check whether the broker deals micro (0.01) and mini (0.1) lots for trading.

- To make knowledgeable trading decisions, it is essential to have the latest market information. Good Forex and CFD brokers will deal with live price facts in their trading platform.

- The next point is having knowledge about the market and how much leverage does the broker offer? If you talk about Europe, in Europe, the brokers should offer access to leverage up to 1:500 for Specialized Clients and 1:30 for Retail Customers.

- What is the least amount a trader needs to start trading? At Admiral Markets, a trader can supply the trading account with as little as €100. This also allows the trader to start small trade without taking a major risk and add as you learn the market psychology and behavior of self-governing trading.

- Admiral Markets can support the trader to decrease his trading risk with volatility defense and negative balance protection.

- Will, the broker, let the trader not simply swing trade, but day trade and scalp as well, if that's a part of the strategy?

- Does the broker in swing trading provide tools and resources to help the beginner to succeed as a trader? As if we talk about Admiral Markets, for example, it has a library of more than hundreds of Forex articles, free courses like Forex 101, and free trading webinars.

Forex Swing Trading Strategies

A Summary

Swing trading is a style suitable for volatile markets, and it also suggests frequent trading chances. Though the trader will need to capitalize a reasonable amount of time into observing the market with swing trading, the supplies are not as difficult as trading styles with smaller time frames, such as day trading or scalping. In calculation, even if you give favor to day trade or scalping, swing trading will offer you few diversifications in your outcomes as well as additional profits. It is said that swing trading is not for all traders, so it is best to practice it with risk-free first with a demo trading account.

Admiral Markets:

Admiral Markets is a market that has attained many successes in the market due to its multi-award-winning achievement. Forex and CFD broker, providing trading on over 8,000 financial instruments via the world's most popular trading platforms:

1. MetaTrader 4

2. MetaTrader 5

This substantial does not hold and should not be construed as containing asset advice, asset recommendations, an offer of or solicitation for any dealings in financial instruments. A beginner should not forget that such trading analysis is not a trustworthy indicator for any current or future performance, as conditions may change over time. Before making any investment conclusions, he should seek guidance from independent financial advisors to confirm that you understand the risks.

4. SWING AND DAY TRADING INDICATORS

What are the indicators of trading?

"Trading indicators are the mathematical calculations, that are designed to predict what market will do."

Trading indicators are plotted as lines on a price chart and may comfort traders to identify certain signals and trends within the market. The number one indicator could be a forecast signal that calculates future price movements, while a lagging indicator looks at past trends and indicates momentum.

Why Are Technical Indicators Important?

Technical indicators are supported algorithms that practice previous price-data in the calculation. As an outcome, all technical indicators of trading are lagging in their natural surroundings, but that doesn't mean that they can't return useful information once day trading the markets. Deprived of the assistance of indicators, traders would have a tough time calculating this volatility of the markets, the strength of a trend, or whether market conditions are overbought or oversold.

That being said, an entire trading strategy shouldn't be dependent solely on technical indicators. They return the simplest results as a confirmation tool. Don't buy just because the RSI is below 30 or sell because the Stochastics oscillator increases directly above 80. As an alternative, a trader should create a definite trading strategy (built on price-action or the fundamentals, for instance) and using technical indicators simply to substantiate a possible setup and modify your entry levels.

Types of Technical Indicators

Depending on the knowledge that technical indicators provide, they'll be grouped into three main categories:

Trend-following indicators.

Momentum indicators.

Volatility indicators.

1. Trend-following indicators

Trend-following indicators are accustomed to determine trends and to live the strong point of a trending market. While most traders are able to identify a trend just by staring at the value chart, it's often difficult to live its strength or to identify a trend early in its establishment. The common trend-following indicators also contain moving averages, MACD, and also the ADX indicator, to call some.

2. Momentum indicator:

It usually measures the strength of recent price-moves relative to previous periods. They vary in the middle of 0 and 100, on condition of the signals of the indicator of overbought and oversold market circumstances. Momentum indicators return a marketing signal when values begin to maneuver strongly higher, and a buying signal when prices start to maneuver strongly lower. While this will be profitable in ranging markets, momentum indicators usually return false signals during strong trends. Some samples of momentum indicators include the RSI, Stochastics, and CCI.

3. Volatility indicators:

Volatility indicators, as per their name recommends, it measures the volatility of the fundamental instrument. Traders are generally chasing volatility from corner to different corner markets to hunt out profitable trading opportunities, which makes volatility indicators a strong tool for day trading. Samples of volatility indicators include Bollinger Bands and also the ATR indicator, among others.

Every investor has faith in the strategy of buying and holding. The only topic of disputation is how long the holding era should last. For every teenager who started buying unappreciated equity and holds it for eight decades, collecting shares along the way, there are dozens of more risk-takers who dearth to get out of their positions in less than a week. This not only requires a stock to rise quickly but also to go up in price high sufficient to offset any matter costs. Swing trading is for the stockholder who factually can't wait for the weekend.

Swing trading is the most fast-paced trading process that is manageable for everyone, even those beginners who have just jumped into the world of trading. The speed of swing trading is slower than day trading, which also delivers the trader with sufficient time to formulate a practice and execute a little research before building decisions on your trade. Swing trading is also a rare method for those looking to create a foray into day trading to increase their skills before embarking on the extra complex day trading process.

Those technical indicators are the mathematical tools that can give actionable info out of a stock plan that can seem uninformed at times. In the hands of an appropriately lucky risk-taker, the right technical indicators can spell a chance for profit. Now, just a rare of the ones most commonly used by swing traders, in ascending order of complexity.

Swing traders tend to have not the same goals as day traders, which goal to pick up on rapid intraday changes due to a catalyst.

Swing trades, on the other hand, tend to goal for "swings" moving from a short-term low back to a new high.

Swing trading signals tend to look not the same as day trading signals. Day traders frequently look for high volatility and volume and look to ride a trend, possibly buying at a pullback to VWAP.

Before we talk about the trading indicators, it is essential to understand what they represent and why and how they represent it are also important questions to think. Swing trading indicators are not better than any other method of technical analysis, and it should certainly not have seen as the divine grail. It is not assured that any trade that a trader makes will yield profit just for the reason that a trading indicator signaled it.

Here are few other factors that can have an influence on whether you end up creating a profit or bearing a loss in swing trading:

- Market Conditions can frequently reduce the effectiveness of indicators. Even if it appears like security is nearby to go up, a broad bearish emotion could cause it to additional fall in value.
- The timing of your trade needs to be rigorous. Receiving the right time can be authoritative to create a huge profit.
- What many people call perception is simply know-how. Like all other things, you will turn out to be a better trader as you spend extra time trading and pick up on subtle market signals.

Swing Trading Indicators:

Swing trade indicators are important to focus on when selecting when to buy when to trade, and what to buy. Some of the top combinations of indicators for swing trading are given below.

1. Moving Averages:

The moving average is one of the foremost basic trading indicators in swing trading. A moving average smoothens erratic short-term price movements and comforts us to better understand the trend and in what way the safety is moving. Moving Averages are good indicators on their own, but they are also used as a base for other, more descriptive indicators. Swing trader should not forget this that moving averages approximately always lag behind the present price thanks to factoring in past data. The more data you think about, the larger the lag. Therefore, as a swing trader. It is smart to mix short term moving averages with longer-term moving averages. Doing so, you think about both the long and short term trend and have more ground on which to base your decisions.

When a trader is observing at moving averages, he will be observing at the calculated lines built on past prices. This indicator is not difficult to understand, and it is also difficult to look at whether you are doing day trading, swing trading, or else even trading longer term. They are used to either confirm a trend or identify a trend. To decide the average, a trader will need to sum up all of the concluding prices as well as the number for days the period covers and then divide the concluding prices via the number of days. To successfully use moving averages, a trader will need to compute different time periods and link them on a chart. This will give the trader a broader lookout of the market, as well as their average changes over time. When you have planned your moving averages, you then must use them to consider in on your trade decisions. You can practice them to:

- **Recognize the Strength of a Trend:**

If the present price of the stock and trend is beyond from its moving average, then it is considered to be a weaker trend. Trend strength, shared by an indicator like volume, can help you create better choices on your trades.

- **Determining Trend Reversals:**

You can use moving averages to recognize trend reversals with limits. You need to watch for instances where the current moving averages cross the longer moving averages after an uptrend. Though this is not the only instrument, you should use to regulate reversal, but it can comfort you to determine whether you should explore it further.

2. Relative Strength Index:

Welles Wilder developed the RSI indicator within the 1970s and distributed his findings in New Concepts in Technical Trading Systems. The book may be a classic text which presented multiple conventional technical indicators like RSI, Average True Range, and, therefore, the Average Directional Index. A simple explanation of RSI's calculation is linking this price strength relative to past price strength. For instance, a 14-period RSI on a daily chart will compare today's price to the last 13 closes. A high reading points out that today's price is powerful, relative to the previous 13 closes, and contrariwise. Wilder planned that RSI could be used as a momentum oscillator: measuring exactly how tough the momentum is during a market, but then RSI came to be used in a different way. RSI is mostly used by the traders as an overbought-oversold indicator, where a great reading means that the stock is "overbought" and is unavoidable for a pullback. In the comparison, an "oversold" reading indicates that the market is due for a rally because it's been sold-off an excessive amount of. This consumption of the indicator compares to the aim of a momentum oscillator, contained by which a great analysis indicates that this trend is further likely to last. In the conventional time series of 14-period RSI is used. The situation is the one suggested in also Wilders' work and is defaulting in maximum charting platforms. On the other hand, the study of Larry Connors's point towards the 14-period RSI comprises a miniature edge, in which shorter-term RSI analyses produce additional commercial signals.

Connors' research indicates that the 2, four, and blended RSI periods show the most effective long-term trade expectation. As a result of his research, Connors developed the Connors RSI indicator (which measures the speed of change of RSI), which is included with most charting packages nowadays.

Relative strength index (RSI) is one of the finest technical indicators for swing trading. This indicator is responsible for giving the information you need to determine once the ideal enters into the market. It allows traders to investigate small signals better. This will help the trader to regulate if the market has been oversold or overbought, is range-bound, or is flat. The RSI will give the trader a relative evaluation of how to secure the existing price by examining both past instability and performance. This indicator will be easily recognized by using a range of 1-100. The RSI indicator is most convenient for:

- **Determining the circumstances that led the market to oversold or overbought:**

A trader will need to be able to classify these conditions so that a trader can find equally trend reversal and corrections. Overbuying can indicate a bearish trend even though overselling can be seen as more bullish. If the indicator is around 30, it could be indicated as an undervalue or oversold. Indicators about 70 may mean that the security was overrated or overbought.

- **Identifying Divergences:**

Divergences are used to classify reversals in trends. When the value hits a new low, but then the RSI does not, then at that time, it would be considered as a bullish divergent signal. If the value hits a new high and the RSI doesn't, then that would be termed a bearish signal.

3. Volume:

A generally overlooked indicator that is easiest for beginners to use, even for new traders, is volume. Looking at volume is very critical when you are considering trends. Trends need to be maintained and supported by volume. A trader always wants to make sure that there is more significant volume going on when the trend is going in that way. Increasing volume means money supporting the safety, and if you do not see the volume, it may possibly be an indication that there are undervalued conditions at play.

4. Visual Analysis Indicator:

Despite the fact that technical indicators for swing trading are critical for making the right choices, it is helpful from many shareholders, both new and experienced, to be able to look at visual patterns. By generating visuals patterns, a trader can see the activities in the market with a quick glance to help support your decision.

5. The Flow of Net Imbalances:

Each day, there are a lot of orders to be found to urge the closing print (market-on-close orders). These are typically institutions like mutual funds and ETFs that need the large liquidity provided at the market close. Some minutes before they close every day, the interactions will distribute information on the order inequalities at the market close. That is, what number more shares are being accepted than sold at the close? For instance, if market-on-close buy orders are equaling 100,000 shares, and sell orders equaling 90,000 shares, that's a +10,000 share imbalance. Market makers arbitrage this within the short-term and make pennies, that's not a timeframe we are able to compete in. However, we are able to track the cash flow of a stock or sector by tracking the trend of the online imbalances over time.

If there are determined in closing the imbalances in one sector, it's indicating that institutions are collecting an edge therein stock. This provides us vital information that a major price move could be on the precipice. The tool I exploit to measure imbalance money flow is Market Chameleon. MC allows you to easily view 20-days or 50-days moving averages of capital inflows and outflows of sectors, industries, indexes, or watch lists.

Day Trading Indicators:

To find the simplest technical indicators for your particular day-trading approach, test out a bunch of them singularly and so together. You will find yourself sticking with, say, four that are evergreen otherwise, you may flip counting on the asset you're trading or the market situations of the day. Regardless of whether you are day-trading stocks, forex, or futures, it's often best to stay it simple when it involves technical indicators. You will find you like viewing only a pair of indicators to endorse entry points and exit points. At most, use simply one from each type of indicator to dodge avoidable and distracting repetition.

Combining Day-Trading Indicators

Consider a combination of sets of two indicators on your expense chart to classify points to initiate and get hold of out of a trade.

For example, Relative strength index RSI and moving average convergence/divergence will be combined on the screen to recommend and strengthen a trading signal. The relative strength index (RSI) can recommend overbought or oversold conditions by measuring the value momentum of an asset. The indicator was produced by J. Welles Wilder Jr, who proposed the momentum reaching 30 (on a scale of zero to 100) was an indication of an asset being oversold, and so a buying chance and a 70 percent level was an indication of an asset is overbought and so a selling or short-selling chance.

Constance Brown, CMT, refined the service of the index and assumed the oversold level in an exceedingly upward-trending market was fundamentally much above 30, and therefore, the overbought level in a downward-trending market was much below 70.3.Using Wilder's levels, the asset price can still trend higher for a few times, whereas the RSI is signifying overbought and the other way around. For that reason, RSI is best monitored only if its signal imitates to the value trend: as an example, hunt for bearish momentum indications when the value trend is bearish and pay no attention to those indications when the value trend is bullish.

To more easily identify those price trends, you'll be able to use the moving average convergence/divergence (MACD) indicator. MACD consists of two chart lines. The MACD line is made by eliminating a 26-period exponential moving average (EMA) from a 12-period EMA. An EMA is that the average value of an asset over a period of your time only with the key change that the foremost recent prices are given greater allowance than prices farther out.

The second line is the signal line and could be a 9-period EMA. A bearish trend is signaled once the MACD line crosses under the signal line; a bullish trend is signaled after the MACD line crosses directly above the signal line.

Choosing Pairs:

While selecting pairs, it is a good knowledge to decide on one indicator that's measured a number one indicator, i.e., RSI and one that's a lagging indicator, i.e., like MACD. Most important indicators make signals before the conditions for entering the trade have arisen. Lagging indicators make warning signs after those circumstances have looked as if, in order that they can act as verification of leading indicators and might prevent you from trading on made-up signals.

A trader must also first-rate a pairing that features indicators as of two of the four different types, never two of the same type. The four types are development like MACD, moments like RSI, volatility, and volume. As their names suggest, volatility indicators are supported volatility within the asset's price, and volume indicators are supported trading volumes of the asset. It's typically not useful to look at two indicators of the identical type since they'll be on condition that the identical information.

Using Multiple Indicators:

A trader might also opt to have live one indicator of every type; it might possibly be two of which are maximum substantial and two of which are lagging. Numerous indicators can provide even more strengthening of trading signals and might increase your probabilities of hunting down made-up signals.

Refining Indicators:

Whatsoever indicators you choose, make sure to research them, and take summaries on their effectiveness over time. Ask yourself: What are an indicator's disadvantages? Does it produce several made-up signals? Does it fail to signal, leading to missed chances? Does it signal too early (more probable of a number one indicator) or too late (more likely of a lagging one)?

You may find one indicator is actual when trading stocks but not, say, forex. You may want to switch out an indicator for an additional one amongst its type or make changes in how it's planned. Making such modifications could be a key part of success when day-trading with technical indicators.

Should You Trade on Technical Indicators?

Technical indicators practice past price-data in their calculation and, as a result, lagging this price. On the other hand, since historical data is that the only piece of knowledge that traders must do in advance for future price movements, technical indicators do have a very important role during a well-defined trading strategy.

Avoiding the addition of too adding too many indicators to your chart as indicators of the identical type generally return similar trading signals. As a replacement for, choose only one indicator out of every group (momentum, trend-following, and volatility) and mix their indications to verify a situation and trade supported it. An efficient mixture of indicators might be the moving be around, the RSI indicator, and, therefore, the ATR indicator, for instance.

Don't base your trading decisions totally on indicators and their signals. Trend-following indicators return a buy signal when prices start to maneuver higher, whether or not the market is trading sideways. In the same way, oscillators and momentum indicators will offer you a marketing signal when prices start to increase during an uptrend. There's no single greatest indicator, which is why you ought to combine different types of indicators and include them into a broader trading strategy.

5. PROS AND CONS OF SWING AND DAY TRADING

Swing trading is far and away one among the foremost popular ways to trade commercial markets. But like any style of strategy, there are both pros and cons when using it, and knowing those prior times may be crucial so as to choose if it's for you within the long term.

Advantages of Swing Trading

- It allows you to require the benefit of the natural ebb and flow of markets. Financial markets never go into one way continually, and by having the ability to require the benefit of that, you'll rise your returns as you, in theory, are visiting be making money once the market rises over the subsequent few days, then make some while the market pulls back, because it will definitely do sooner or later.

- By actuality in and out of the markets, you'll identify more chances. If you study any economic chart, you'll see that there's nearly always a precise long-term trend, but the market may not continuously be at a sustenance or resistance area. By being in an exceedingly and out of the market in a matter of some days (typically), you'll collect profits and identify other markets that are putting in for other trades. This enables you to spread the danger around and ties up lots less capital rather than continually having to come back up with margin for brand spanking new positions as you discover new trades. By closing your first position, you'll not deposit extra money in your account to hide the second.

- Stop losses are typically smaller than long-run trades. The stop losses on a swing trade may well be 100 pips based upon a four-hour chart, while a stop loss on a weekly chart that's based upon the trend might need to be 400 pips. This enables you to put larger sized positions rather than extremely low leveraged ones via the longer-term trends.

- You've got clear boundaries. The swing trader could be an extra technical based trader, and per se will normally have a particular area that they deem as being an indication the trade is functioning against them. Due to this, you recognize exactly when the trade isn't working and may limit the damage a nasty trade can do. Longer-term traders normally must provide a wide berth for the markets as they look forward to them to "go with the fundamentals."

Disadvantages of Swing Trading

- You will get whipsawed often, simply because the market shows support or resistance at a particular area, doesn't mean they'll be respecting it today. Also, anytime you can place a trade, you're risking money. Due to this, as a swing trader, you're risking it more often. Odds are you'll have losses from time to time, irrespective of how good you're.

- You will get to be knowledgeable in technical analysis. Whereas not necessarily a "disadvantage," it means extra work. Nearly any person can tell the trend on a chart that's going from the lower left to the upper right over time, but someone was trying to swing trade that a chart must identify entry and exit points. This is often something a technical analysis can do, but you would have to tell about it first. This takes time.

- It takes a unique mindset than long-run trading and more nerves. While it isn't necessarily scalping, the swing trader does run the danger of being "alarmed out of the markets" as pullbacks in these lesser ranges appear to be more violent than to someone observing a weekly chart. This is often a psychological issue and one that the majority of traders will eventually accommodate during their careers.

As you'll see, there are pros and cons to swing trading, a bit like the rest. To be honest, most traders do a touch of varied different styles because the markets aren't necessarily always conducive to at least one particular style of trading and sometimes can involve others. An honest trader is able to use various styles of trading so as to extend their funds. The trader must befit the markets, not the opposite way around.

Swing Trading Example:

Find a stock in the market that has been trading in the direction of the upside for the past week, and has prepared short & sharp bottoms on its daily chart. Also, determine the stock's performance since the uptrend started and note if its price refunded to the moving average thrice. If it did, and also penetrated the moving average at a median of 1.5% of its price, a good buy order may be placed. This order may be approximately 1% of the stock's price below the moving average.

When the trade has been moving, it's advisable to put a stop loss near the entry point to curb losses. And profits may be taken near the upper channel line for weak markets, and at the upper station line, for strong markets. The purpose is to take profits in line with your trading plan, but an expert trader may favor holding for ages longer till when the market doesn't visit new highs.

Advantages of Day Trading:

Trading strategy:

Day trading lets you use a range of trading strategies across all major markets. Common day trading strategies contain breakout trading, counter-trend trading, and trend-following (or mean-reversion). In breakout trading, traders try and catch the early volatility that happens instantaneously after the worth breaks a very important technical level, like chart patterns. Incomplete orders tend to bunch above and below important levels, which ends up in a flow in momentum and volatility after the worth hits those levels and triggers the undecided orders. Breakout trading also lets day traders line an incomplete order to catch a breakout once it happens, as pending orders become market orders once the worth reaches the pre-specified level. Popular technical tools employed by breakout traders contain chart patterns, like head and shoulders patterns, triangles, double tops and bottoms, triple tops and bottoms, rectangles, wedges, and flags. Additionally, breakout traders also can make the most of the volatility that happens after the worth breaks above or below a channel, trend line, or horizontal funding or resistance levels. Trend-following strategies, as their name proposes, include opening day trades within the direction of the underlying intra-day trend. Trend-following is probably the foremost popular trading strategy among day traders because it returns a lovely risk-to-reward ratio with a comparatively high success rate. To open exchange the way of the underlying trend, await the worth to finish a pullback (e.g., to a very important intraday Fibonacci level) and use candlestick patterns to form sure the underlying trend is on the point of continue.

Counter-trend trading strategies include opening trades within the other way of the underlying trend. Counter-trend trader's goal to catch market corrections that occur after a chronic and powerful uptrend or downtrend. This trading strategy is slightly riskier than breakout trading and trend-following and may be used only by knowledgeable day traders.

More Trading Opportunities:

Since day trading could be a relatively fast-paced trading style, it offers an outsized number of trading opportunities – on a daily basis. Day traders base their choices totally on intraday timeframes, like the 15-min, 30-min, 1-hour, and 4-hour ones. Those timeframes offer way more tradeable setups than the daily or weekly charts employed by swing traders and position traders, which could be a major advantage of day trading.

However, keep in mind that shorter-term timeframes usually contain more market noise, which might quickly accumulate losses if you set your stop-loss levels too tight. To avoid this, try and measure the typical volatility of the security that you are trading (by means of the ATR indicator, for instance), and place your stop losses for that reason.

An advanced amount of trading chances doesn't essentially mean more income. A trader should follow your trading plan and only place those trades that are completely in-line with your strategy. Risk management also plays a very important role in day trading success, so confirm to risk a little percentage of your trading account on any single trade.

Higher Trading Costs:

Even though day trading the market, you'll have greater trading costs than once swing or position trading the market. Since day trading contains opening more trades throughout the day, choose a broker that has tight spreads and low trading fees. Some brokers offer stable spreads, which might be exciting for traders who want to trade around significant news releases and retain trading costs low. News releases tend to steer to high market slippage, volatility, higher trading costs, which are a few things you wish to grasp if you're about to trade important market reports. Within the long term, those trading costs can quickly add up and reduce your profits.

Limited Profit Potential:

Assumed the shorter holding periods of trades and shorter timeframes on which day traders base their choices, day trading includes a more restricted profit potential linked to swing trading. Additionally, traders close their trades by the tip of the trading day irrespective of their profit. While this practice removes overnight risk, it also limits the probable profits of promising trade setups.

Risk of Overleveraging Your Trades:

Most markets don't change much over the day. As a result, day traders utilize more leverage to squeeze out the foremost profits and make the most of these small price actions. While leverage is often very efficient, traders who over-leverage their trades also risk larger losses.

Leverage may be a double-edged sword and will be used only per your trading plan to ensure to make a strict risk management attempt to cap your influence or risk-per-trade in such how that removes the danger of ruin (i.e., blowing your account.)

Market Noise

The shorter the timeframe, you're trading on the more market noise you've got to handle. Market noise represents unpredictable and unpredictable price behavior with none technical reasoning or news that would have led to those movements. Market noise presents a true problem for short-term traders, and therefore the only thanks to avoiding getting stopped out too early are to widen your stop-loss level. Take a glance at the previous volatility within the pair, and take a look at to line your stop-loss above or below recent support and resistance levels, giving the market sufficient space to perform.

CONCLUSION

Swing trading is extremely popular because it is administrated on higher time-frame charts allowing a trader to trade the markets, hold down employment, study, or do other things with their time. It may also be accustomed to capture the big intraday moves for the traders who are looking to trade within the sessions and don't want to carry trades overnight or for extended periods of time. This is only one trading strategy of the many traders who can have their own toolbox. Before deciding if it's for you, confirm your test and excellent it on a demo trading account.

A trader should be disciplined and rigorous to start out day trading. A typical day trader problem is that they act and deviate from their strategy. Sometimes you can pass before you realize you're not strictly following your initial strategy. This will trouble the victory rate of the strategy and breaks the odds. An honest thanks to tackling discipline issues is to jot down the precise rules of your strategy and stick the note to your monitor so it'll always be ahead of you during trading sessions. This way, you'll continually be reminded to follow your strategy rules. In each of the above trades, we've carefully calculated the end result. You ought to do so, too, to be conversant in what exactly can happen to you in every trade. When you get extra established, it gets easier, and a few progressive day trading apps also will calculate everything for you spontaneously. Although being different to day trading, reviews and results propose swing trading could also be a nifty system for beginners to start out with. This can be due to the intraday that changes dozens of securities can be proven too hectic. Whereas swing traders will see their earnings within a pair of days, keeping motivation levels high. At the identical time vs. long-term trading, swing trading is brief enough to stop interruption.

www.ingramcontent.com/pod-product-compliance
Lightning Source LLC
Chambersburg PA
CBHW071752240526
45465CB00031B/612